MW01078401

USE THIS
IF YOU WANT
TO TAKE GREAT
PHOTOGRAPHS.

A photo journal

HENRY
CARROLL

Is this you?

You own a decent camera, maybe it's a phone or a swanky DSLR, you have a good grasp of the technical stuff and your sense of composition is pretty tuned in, too. But here's the thing – sometimes you feel a little short on ideas and inspiration.

All the photography greats have felt the same way at some point. That's because taking great photographs isn't just about good cameras and technical knowhow. There's a whole other side to it and that's exactly what this book is going to help you with.

Inside you'll find short 'creative springboards' and some handy technical tips should you need a little extra help. These springboards are there to spark your imagination. Dip in, dip out or start at the beginning and work your way through to the end. It's totally up to you.

There's only one correct solution to a creative problem – your solution.

This isn't about 'right' or 'wrong' answers and you're free to interpret these springboards in any way you want. Some are pretty straightforward, others a bit weird. Some you'll love, others not so much. That's all part of the fun, and figuring out which ones you respond to best will lead you to your own distinctive photographic voice.

How to use this book

This book encourages you to print your pictures and stick them in so you make your own, really personal photobook. You don't have to do this, but printing your pictures makes them into something physical and precious and this is a very important part of developing your photography.

I recommend printing on 4 x 6-inch (or 100 x 150-mm) photo paper either at home or at a lab. Experiment with gloss and matte finishes to see what suits a picture best. You can then use the sticky corners provided or spray glue to fix your pictures to the page.

In the back of the book you'll find some pointers, but don't treat these like the right answers, because how you interpret these springboards is totally up to you. These pages also double as an index to remind you what inspired your pictures.

#UseThisPhotoBook

Post your pictures on Instagram using the hashtag #UseThisPhotoBook to receive feedback and see what everyone else has done!

**Photograph your
earliest memory.**

**Go somewhere really
touristy and take
non-touristy pictures.**

Laser vision

Jesse Marlow

2011

It may look like a lucky shot, but
Marlow would have been ready and
waiting for this woman to walk into the
frame and complete his joke. It's the
result of an acute visual awareness of the
layers created in an image by foreground
and background.

Tell a joke with
a single picture.

**Take an ugly picture
of something beautiful.**

**Take a beautiful picture
of something ugly.**

Take a political
photograph of nature.

Mono Lake
Robert Voit
California, USA, 2006

A tree stands tall from a forest of pines. Only this particular tree is not a product of nature, it's one of man – a giant cellular phone mast casting radioactive wavelengths through the fresh mountain air. This failed attempt at imitating 'treeness' is comically absurd. Rather than being respectful, its presence only highlights our misaligned relationship with the natural world.

How are you feeling?
Communicate
this with light.

Take a picture
that helps you come
to terms with a
personal hang-up.

from the series 'Field Trip'
Martin Kollar
Israel, 2009–11

Function takes precedence over
form when building a roadblock, but
here each object seems to have been
meticulously placed. It's Kollar's
choice of camera angle and framing
that accentuates the beauty of this
inadvertent artwork. It causes that
central barrel to play with our sense
of scale and space.

**Show beauty
in the banal.**

**Photograph the
last thing that
made you laugh.**

**And what about the
last thing that
made you cry?**

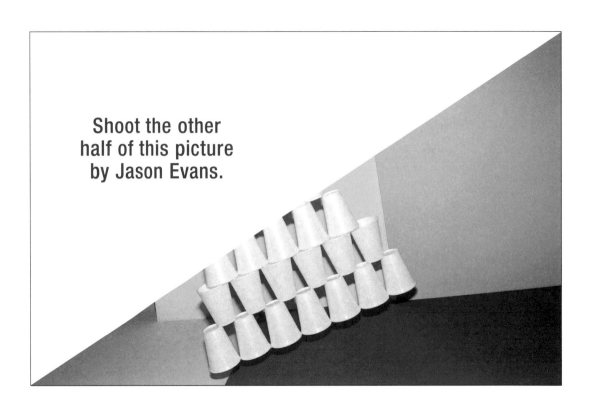

Shoot the other
half of this picture
by Jason Evans.

Take the best picture you can. Right now.

**Make something
big look small.**

**Make something
small look big.**

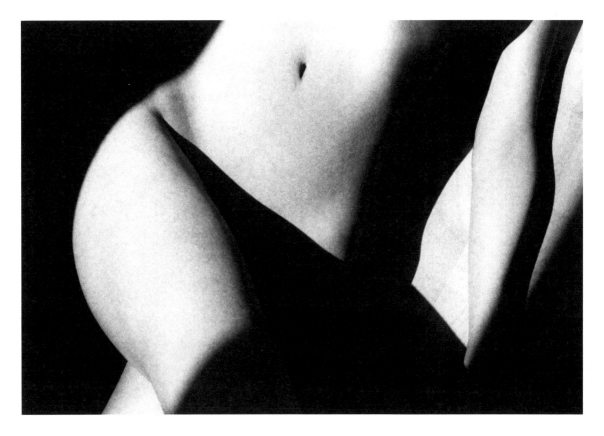

Untitled
Ralph Gibson
2007

This model may be nude, but that
shadow preserves her modesty as
effectively as clothing. Gibson uses hard
light with black and white to abstract the
human form. So dense are the resulting
shadows that they feel like ever present
forms in their own right.

**Photograph
a shadow.**

**Throw something
at your subject
and capture their
reaction with a
fast shutter speed.**

People whose opinion I respect when it comes to my photography:

....

....

....

....

....

....

....

....

....

Gilles Peress

Tabriz, Iran

1980

In his series 'Telex Iran', Peress
captures a country in the midst
of revolution. In this unorthodox
composition heads are cut in half
by the edge of frame and people look
this way and that. Decisive change is
afoot, but Peress depicts a fragmented
society with no clear sense of
unity or direction.

**Create drama
around the edge
of your frame.**

Recreate a famous photograph without looking it up.

Imagine you're Elvis.
What was your
final photograph?

Elliott Erwitt

Cannes, France

1975

An old couple while away their golden
years before being carried away by
the breeziness of time. Two identical
pictures, side by side, with one obvious
difference. It's the perfect visual
set up and punch line. So precise is
Erwitt's joke, any additional written
explanation seems futile.

Tell a joke...

...with two pictures.

**Contrast movement
and stillness in
a single frame.**

Cover your screen
with black tape.
Spend the day shooting
and only remove
the tape when
you get home.

**Take a picture
that looks beautiful
against this colour.**

And this.

**Use shutter speed
to capture anger.**

Use aperture to
capture melancholy.

**Take a picture
that only works
in colour.**

Untitled
from the series 'A City in the Mind'
Peter Fraser
2012

It's a conch. Nothing unusual there. It's
just that this particular shell seems so
… I don't know … 'sexy'. Those lascivious
pinks seduce us into having a carnal
encounter with an everyday object.
Fraser's picture serves as a reminder
that nothing is ordinary and nothing
should be overlooked.

**Create a playlist.
Now listen to it while
out taking pictures.**

Shoot one
more image for
Robert Frank's
'The Americans'.

Livia

Frederick Sommer

1948

Livia is her name and she looks all the
more fresh faced when set against that
peeling backdrop. But tonal similarities
mean she both emerges and retreats.
This is a complex portrait by Sommer,
who uses black and white to remind us
that no one escapes the passage of time.

Take a picture that
only works in
black and white.

Take us on a journey
through your picture.

**Take a beautiful
picture that follows no
compositional rules.**

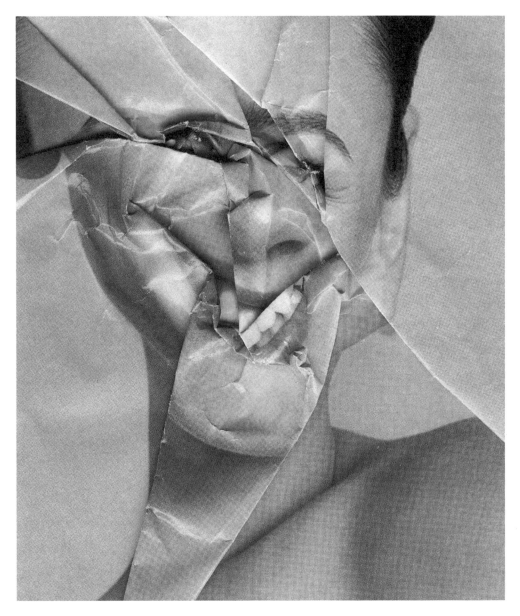

Through the violent act of crumpling
pages of glossy magazines,
Shanabrook and Georgieva cause the
'perfect' faces of models to look more
like hideous monsters. In so doing,
they morph the ubiquitous notion of
mass-media beauty into something
far more unique and characterful.

Re-photograph
a photograph
to change its
original meaning.

**Take a photograph
that whispers.**

Take a photograph
that shouts.

**A record of
missed photo
opportunities.**

Capture someone's
subconscious.

~T.H.O.H.Y~_xXxKIRAxXx_Black Shot
Mintio
2010

This Singaporean teenager is totally lost in the addictive world of virtual shoot'em ups. Mintio's use of artificial lighting and double exposure presents her subject in a kind of narcotic limbo land between reality and artifice.

'I am at war with the obvious.'

William Eggleston

Join Eggleston's war.

**Use framing to
create a photograph
within a photograph.**

A street in Beijing as seen from inside an antique dealer's shop

Marc Riboud

1965

By photographing through the windows of a shop, Riboud breaks up a street scene into six vignettes. The people occupy the same space, but the framing means we view everything in isolation. Curious gazes become intensified and fleeting gestures take on more significance.

Take a picture of
yourself pretending to
be someone else.

Take a picture of
yourself pretending to
be yourself.

**Take a picture of
yourself as yourself.**

Photograph
a park bench.
On the opposite page
give it a title
which changes our
understanding
of the image.

Make light the subject
of your photograph.

Untitled Polaroid
Mike Slack
2009

Armed with a Polaroid camera, Mike
Slack responds to the intensity of the
Californian sun by creating beautiful
square-format haikus. Here a slice of
daylight inches its way across the corner
of a nondescript room, like a geometric
slug minding its own business.

Head out with a
fellow photographer
and play a game of
photography dare.

Take a picture
that breaks your worst
photography habit.

**Make a sequence of
four photos inspired
by the rise and fall of
Britney Spears
(or another celebrity).**

**Let a window do
all the talking.**

CERTAIN WORDS MUST BE SAID

Things had become impossible between them, and nothing could be salvaged.
        Certain words must be said. And although each one had said those words
a hundred times to herself, they never had the courage to say them out loud
to one another.
So they began to hope someone else might say the necessary words for them.
Perhaps a letter might arrive or a telegram sent that would say what they couldn't.
        Now they spent their days waiting. What else could they do?

Certain Words Must Be Said
Duane Michals
1987

Natural light cuts through the room
setting a disquieting tone. Are these
women friends, sisters or lovers?
Even with the handwritten annotation
their relationship remains unclear.
Michals is a master of melancholy
and his work helps us come to terms
with life's most intimate questions.

**Take a picture of
something you hate.**

Email it to
ihatethis@henrycarroll.co.uk.
I'll email you back a picture
of something I hate.

Henri Cartier-Bresson

Alicante, Spain

1933

First we follow the woman's arm on the
left to a razor, which hovers menacingly
near the central figure's neck. From
there we drop down her arm and rise
up again to the touching hands. Here
we encounter another point of tension
in that face, before being guided out of
frame by the sloping arm on the right.
Beautiful, isn't it?

**Turn form
into rhythm.**

A record of interesting
backgrounds that I can
return to later should
I need to shoot
someone's portrait.

Twenty Past Nine

Panos Kokkinias

2010

As night takes hold in Kokkinias'
photograph the sky turns threatening
and the fading daylight succumbs to
artificial sources. Who is the couple
in the kitchen? Their conversation and
body language seem forced. It's twenty
past nine and one of them has brought
home bad news, but it's not clear if it's
him or if it's her.

Instil a powerful
sense of narrative
in your picture.

**Photograph a place
that's nondescript
during the day...**

...but comes
alive at night.

**Next time you
pass something that
makes you think,
*'hey, that would
make a great picture',*
actually stop and
take a picture.**

My photography book wish list:

....

....

....

....

....

....

....

....

....

**Show us the
world is flat.**

Imaginary Landscape
Franco Fontana
Puglia, 1995

By excluding the horizon line and
employing the flattening effects of
a telephoto lens, Fontana removes
any sense of depth and gives this
Italian landscape the feel of an
abstract painting.

Photograph a lie.

Photograph the truth.

**Use exposure
as a metaphor.**

The Three Hags of the Promontory
Amelia Stein
2014–15

Atlantic waves forever pound the cliffs
of northwest Ireland. Stein captures the
psychology of this landscape with dark,
brooding tones. Rock faces ebb into
blackness while murky water churns
at their base. What shadowy tales of
suicides and smugglers do these cliffs
have to tell, I wonder?

**Take a picture inspired
by a line from your
favourite poem.**

**Create ambiguity
with a blend of natural
and artificial light.**

Sancti Spiritus
Alex Webb
Cuba, 1993

In the foreground two boys linger in
a hue of green. In the distance a man
stands tall against an orange sky.
Between them, a pool of light causes
two girls to emerge from the shadows.
This may well be a benign scene, but
the transitioning light creates
an undercurrent of unease.

**Walk down a busy
street taking pictures
without stopping.**

How close can
you get to someone
without your presence
being felt?

Mosh

Elaine Constantine

1997

Flash isn't just about illuminating a
subject. It can also be used to freeze
movement. Here, Constantine's
trademark use of flash crystallizes the
adolescent action. And thank God for
that, or we'd be wiping the spray of
hormones from our faces.

**Use flash to capture
the energy of a party.**

Photograph an
animal as though
it were a human.

Photograph a
human as though
it were an animal.

Take a group portrait
that captures
the individuality
of each subject.

*The Dining Room
(Francis Place)*

Sarah Jones
1997

The girls are close friends and they
are pictured in one of their homes.
But far from being an informal portrait
of youth, the girls' disconnection
from each other and their imposing
surroundings creates tension.
Any hint of childhood frivolity has
been quashed by whatever socially
oppressive traditions are bearing
down on them.

Photograph a sound.

Find an object,
close your eyes
and compose your shot
using touch rather
than vision.

Untitled
Luke Butterly
2014

Who do these clothes belong to
and what circumstances caused
their owner to take off? Butterly's
photograph is full of clues that hint
at the person behind the possessions,
but ultimately it's up to us to build an
image of them in our minds.

Make a portrait of
someone without them
being in the picture.

Keep walking
until you are lost.
Take a photograph
the moment you realize
you are lost.

Take a photograph
that could only
be taken today,
not yesterday
or tomorrow.

Email one of
your pictures to
your photography hero
and ask them what they
don't like about it.

....

doesn't like this picture because:

....

....

....

....

....

....

....

....

....

Untitled

Walker Evans

1928–30

It's the late 1920s, a time when the
Great Depression was about to cripple
a nation. Evans' photograph transforms
a single word into a powerful metaphor
and 'DAMAGED' becomes a sign of the
times. These workmen might as well be
lifting the whole of America onto the
back of that truck.

Photograph a word to
change its meaning.

Sit in one spot
for five hours.
Only take pictures
when the light is at
its most beautiful.

**Compose a picture
with the intention
of displaying it
upside down.**

Take a picture inspired
by the last thing that
jolted you awake.

Photograph a
vegetable so it looks
like a body part.

Mask XCI
John Stezaker
2009

A scenic road projects out from the 'eye' of a Hollywood hottie like the death stare of a Cyclops, while a tunnel through the rock provides a borehole into her mind. Stezaker is a welder of images. Here his precise fusing technique alters the purpose of the original components and gives birth to a new, singular entity.

Combine two
images to create
something surreal.

Shoot an advert where
the image says it all
without the need for
any additional copy.

Freeze the frame
exactly 57 minutes
and 32 seconds in to
your favourite film.
Take a picture inspired
by what you see.

Sit opposite someone
for two hours.
Chat, have a cuppa,
but only take
pictures when you see
something revealing.

Turn a DSLR into
a pinhole camera.

Lula Hand
Florencia Durante
2006

The glowing yellow orb encircling
the sitter's hand is like an apparition,
but a benign one, as though it's the
visualization of someone's aura. Durante
'paints' with light using LEDs and
shutter speeds of around five seconds.
She then follows up with a soft flash to
illuminate the whole scene.

Show us that
photography is a
form of magic.

**Take a picture by the
light of a full moon.**

Don't take any
more photographs
– none –
until you see
something that
emotionally moves you.
Only then pick up
your camera.

Tips and index

25
People whose opinion I respect when it comes to my photography.

Who are the people you trust to give you honest, constructive criticism because they totally get you and your pictures? These are the people to listen to and no one else.

27
Create drama around the edge of your frame.

Rather than positioning subjects comfortably within your frame, place them around the peripheries. This throws off the balance and creates drama, especially if you use a wide-angle lens.

28
Recreate a famous photograph without looking it up.

Often a small detail in an image, like a distinctive hand gesture or facial expression, holds our fascination more so than the whole scene. What detail from your chosen image has lodged itself in your mind? Start there.

29
Imagine you're Elvis. What was your final photograph?

Get into the mind of Elvis in his final hours. What was he thinking and feeling – regret, loneliness, shame…? Complete The King's story.

31
Tell a joke with two pictures.

A single picture can't tell a story as it has no beginning or end. Two (or more) pictures can. The images might not do anything on their own, but when placed next to each other, that's when the magic happens.

32
Contrast movement and stillness in a single frame.

Use a slow shutter speed and remember to mount your camera on a tripod – otherwise camera shake will make everything look blurred.

33
Cover your screen with black tape. Spend the day shooting and only remove the tape when you get home.

Looking at your pictures as soon as you take them is like taking your eye off the ball. Breaking this habit will fine-tune your eyes. You'll see things that you were otherwise blind to.

34–35
Take a picture that looks beautiful against these colours.

'Complimentary colours' pop against each other because they are opposites – green and red, orange and blue, yellow and purple. This creates impact. 'Analogous colours' lie next to each other on the colour wheel – green and yellow, red and orange, blue and purple. This creates harmony. Experiment!

36–37
Use shutter speed to capture anger.
Use aperture to capture melancholy.

Adjusting shutter speed and aperture isn't just about finding the correct exposure. They each create distinctive visual effects that can be used expressively to manipulate mood and emotion.

38
Take a picture that only works in colour.

Tune in to the different emotions that colours can provoke. Reds can be quite dramatic, blues carry a sense of unease and yellows are upbeat.

40
Create a playlist. Now listen to it while out taking pictures.

Choose your tunes wisely, as listening to music affects your headspace and changes how you see and photograph the world.

41
Shoot one more image for Robert Frank's 'The Americans'.

Loneliness, cultural uncertainty, social tension. These are just some of the things that Frank manages to capture in his grainy black-and-white photographs of people and places.

43
Take a picture that only works in black and white.

Black and white draws out tones, textures and surfaces. Have more control over tonal range by shooting RAW and converting your picture to black and white later using image-processing software.

44
Take us on a journey through your picture.

Leading lines, layering and framing are compositional devices that lead the viewer through your picture from foreground to background. This helps to create depth.

45
Take a beautiful picture that follows no compositional rules.

Rule of thirds, foreground interest and lead room. These are essential techniques, but they can feel a little 'off the shelf'. Finding your own distinctive style often means breaking a few rules.

47
Re-photograph a photograph to change its original meaning.

You could re-photograph a picture to crop out part of the original scene. You could re-photograph it in a contrasting context. You could paint on it or rip it up – anything you like!

48–49
Take a photograph that whispers.
Take a photograph that shouts.

Think about black and white tonal range or colour saturation. What's the appropriate size? Are you freezing a moment or capturing something slower? What about the lighting and the different effects of natural versus artificial?

50–51
A record of missed photo opportunities.

You can't photograph everything. Maybe it's because you didn't have your camera with you or a moment came and went too quickly. Happens to us all. The main thing is to always be looking, because using your eyes is the key to all great photographs.

52
Capture someone's subconscious.

By giving your subject something to do they become less aware of the act of being photographed and their subconscious takes over.

54–55
'I am at war with the obvious.'
William Eggleston

Join Eggleston's war.

Sunsets, pretty flowers and beaches. These are 'obvious' subjects offering a conventional idea of beauty. Instead, hunt down more unusual, surprising subjects – the sort that only come alive when they are photographed.

56
Use framing to create a photograph within a photograph.

Framed elements should act like photographs in their own right, like mini compositions within your composition. So it's important to find subjects worth framing.

58–59
Take a picture of yourself pretending to be someone else.

Take a picture of yourself pretending to be yourself.

Take a picture of yourself as yourself.

For part one look at Cindy Sherman, Aneta Grzeszykowska and Yasumasa Morimura. For part two look at your own Facebook page. For part three look at Lee Friedlander, Jen Davis and Nan Goldin.

60
Photograph a park bench. On the opposite page give it a title which changes our understanding of the image.

Almost all images come with some kind of text. This extra context, whether a date, place name, hashtag or something less literal, alters how we read the image. Have a play and get a feel for how words affect images.

62
Make light the subject of your photograph.

Use Exposure Compensation ☒ to vary the appearance of the light. Scroll towards the + to overexpose. Scroll towards the – to underexpose.

64
Head out with a fellow photographer and play a game of photography dare.

With the support of a like-minded friend you'll push yourself further outside your comfort zone. Maybe pick someone from your list on page 25.

65
Take a picture that breaks your worst photography habit.

Maybe you don't get close enough. Maybe you think, 'I can fix that later'. Maybe you tend to justify why a mediocre picture has merit. Maybe you overcook your pictures in post. We all have our bad habits that we need to keep in check.

66–67
Make a sequence of four pictures inspired by the rise and fall of Britney Spears (or another celebrity).

The key to all great photo-sequences is knowing what moments, whether macro or micro, to build your narrative around. Sketch out your story and plan each picture before you start shooting.

68
Let a window do all the talking.

Windows are metaphorical. They allow us to see out or see in. They are openings that can offer freedom or confinement. Windows also fill interior space with beautiful natural light, which lends images a sense of honesty.

70–71
Take a picture of something you hate.
Email it to ihatethis@henrycarroll.co.uk and I'll email you back a picture of something I hate.

You could photograph your subject in such a way as to communicate your hatred. Alternatively, you could take a more matter-of-fact, neutral approach. I suppose it depends on what you hate and why!

73
Turn form into rhythm.

Try to dissociate what you are seeing from what your subject actually is – a chair is not a chair, a body is not a body. Instead, see the world as a collection of shapes, colour, light and space.

74–75
A record of interesting backgrounds that I can return to later should I need to shoot someone's portrait.

Don't worry about the pictures being 'good'. These are simply snaps that serve as your personal catalogue to reference later.

77
Instil a powerful sense of narrative in your picture.

When constructing a scene, think about what each element is saying. If there's a packet of cigarettes on the table, what's the brand? If a picture hangs on the wall, what does it show? The French call this *mise en scène*, and so do the rest of us.

78–79
Photograph a place that's nondescript during the day…
…but comes alive at night.

The city's daily transition from natural to artificial light means grey concrete becomes luminous at night under the glow of streetlights, neon signs and shop windows.

80
Next time you pass something and think, *'hey, that would make a great picture'*, actually stop and take a picture.

'I haven't got time', 'I can't pull over', 'I've got the wrong camera'. All excuses! Photo-ops need to be seized or you regret it forever.

81
My photography book wish list.

You can't take great photographs without surrounding yourself with great photographs. You can look things up online, but nothing replaces the power of a picture on a page.

82
Show us the world is flat.

A long focal length (telephoto lens) will compress, or foreshorten, the space between the foreground and background. This causes images to look flat or more graphic.

84–85
Photograph a lie.
Photograph the truth.

Subject matter, framing and the precise moment you press the shutter are all creative choices. These choices either add up to the truth or a lie. What are you trying to say and why?

86
Use exposure as a metaphor.

Use Exposure Compensation ☒ to either underexpose or overexpose your image.

88–89
Take a picture inspired by a line from your favourite poem.

Capture the poem's mood by making use of light and location. Think about how you could use depth of field or shutter speed emotively. What would be best – black and white or colour?

90
Create ambiguity with a blend of natural and artificial light.

Use White Balance (**WB**) to manipulate the colour of light, or, for more control, set your camera to Auto White Balance (**AWB**) and tweak the colours afterwards using image-processing software.

92
Walk down a busy street taking pictures without stopping.

This technique means you can move quicker, shoot from the hip and capture people unawares. Stick to one focal length and get a feel for the field of view it offers so you can visualize the frame without having to look through your camera.

93
How close can you get to someone without your presence being felt?

It's amazing how closed off people on the street can be. Move slow, pretend to look elsewhere, edge closer and pull your camera up at the very last moment.

95
Use flash to capture the energy of a party.

Avoid using shutter speeds faster than **1/200** as this will be faster than your camera's 'flash sync speed'. This means your shutter will not be fully open when the flash fires, leading to part of your picture being underexposed.

96–97
Photograph an animal as though it were a human.
Photograph a human as though it were an animal.

For animals, camera angle, concentrating on the eyes and lighting will help the viewer to feel empathy. For people, someone's inner animal often reveals itself during moments of physical exertion, anger or pain.

98
Take a group portrait that captures the individuality of each subject.

When posing people, you can either put them in positions which make them feel disconnected (as Sarah Jones does) or group them together and then wait a while before taking the picture so everyone naturally starts to do their own thing.

100
Photograph a sound.

What techniques, like shutter speed or ISO, could visually represent sound? (Photographing something that makes a sound isn't photographing a sound!)

101
Find an object, close your eyes and compose your shot using touch rather than vision.

To communicate something's three-dimensional qualities in a two-dimensional image you need to appreciate its form rather than function.

103
Make a portrait of someone without them being in the picture.

A great portrait should be 'about' someone, but not necessarily 'of' someone. What can you tell about a person by their possessions and the traces they leave behind?

104
Keep walking until you are lost. Take a photograph the moment you realize you are lost.

Getting lost leads you to unexpected subjects and encounters. Leave your phone, money and ID at home and let your camera be your only security. But don't blame me if you never find your way home, OK?

105
Take a photograph that could only be taken today, not yesterday or tomorrow.

Is today an anniversary – happy or sad? Are you visiting somewhere significant – do you want to or have to? Received news – good or bad? This could be one of those very personal pictures that makes sense only to you. And that's fine.

106–107
Email one of your pictures to your photography hero and ask them what they don't like about it.

Ask someone what they like about your pictures and you'll receive all sorts of compliments. That's nice, but you won't learn anything. By asking someone what they don't like about your pictures you'll be made aware of things you haven't even considered.

109
Photograph a word to change its meaning.

We're surrounded by words. These words make sense because we see them in context, but when isolated in the frame their meaning becomes more ambiguous.

110
Sit in one spot for five hours. Only take pictures when the light is at its most beautiful.

Sometimes you get lucky with light, but more often than not it's a waiting game. If you're into landscapes, patience is the price you pay for a great picture.

111
Compose a picture with the intention of displaying it upside down.

Use your eyes as weighing scales to constantly size up the relative 'visual weights' of elements within your frame and create absolute balance.

112
Take a picture inspired by the last thing that jolted you awake.

Waking up suddenly is usually prompted by a dramatic mental image involving movement, like something flying towards you or falling suddenly. Use shutter speed to capture this intense movement in your photograph.

113
Photograph a vegetable so it looks like a body part.

Depending on the colour of your vegetable, you might find that black and white helps to abstract it. You might also compose your photograph so that you're not showing the whole vegetable.

115
Combine two images to create something surreal.

Collect images, be playful and embrace the element of chance. Lay them out and shuffle them around. Intuitively respond to line, shape and scale. Surprise yourself with the peculiarity of pictures!

116
Shoot an advert where the image says it all without the need for any additional copy.

First you need a concept that captures what sets the product apart. Then think about every single element of your image, from colours to composition to lighting. The picture needs to be as precise as a sentence.

117
Freeze the frame exactly 57 minutes and 32 seconds in to your favourite film. Take a picture inspired by what you see.

There's something creatively liberating about arriving at an image through a process that's out of your control. This element of chance can open up a whole world of new ideas!

118
Sit opposite someone for two hours. Chat, have a cuppa, but only take pictures when you see something revealing.

Use a tripod and sit next to your camera, not behind it. Also use a cable release or remote. Both these techniques help you build a more personal connection with your subject.

119
Turn a DSLR into a pinhole camera.

Drill a hole into the camera's body cap (not while it's on the camera!).

With a needle, make a small hole in the centre of a 2x2-cm (¾x¾-in) piece of kitchen foil and tape it onto the body cap.

Screw the body cap onto camera and try taking pictures with slow shutter speeds.

121
Show us that photography is a form of magic.

The great thing about painting with light is that you never know exactly what you're going to get. Keep note of exact timings and movements so you can perfect your technique from one picture to the next.

122
Take a picture by the light of a full moon.

If you experiment with long shutter speeds, you'll find that night turns to day. Use the Bulb (**B**) setting on your camera for shutter speeds longer than 30 seconds.

123
Don't take any more photographs – none – until you see something that emotionally moves you. Only then pick up your camera.

To take great photographs you need to respond to your instincts and feed off your emotions. This isn't about being moved to tears. You might respond to something simple, like a particular quality of light.

I'd like to thank the following people who helped me in the making of this book:

Picture Credits

6 Courtesy of M.33, Melbourne / **11** Courtesy Robert Voit / **14** Image courtesy of the artist / **18** Untitled from *I Feel Love* (2004), courtesy Jason Evans / **22** Image courtesy and © Ralph Gibson / **26** © Gilles Peress/Magnum Photos / **30** © Elliott Erwitt/Magnum Photos / **39** From the series 'A City in the Mind' (Steidl Verlag) / **42** © Frederick & Frances Sommer Foundation / **46** Digital c-print from crumpled magazine page, image courtesy of the artists / **53** Courtesy Mintio / **57** © Marc Riboud/Magnum Photos / **63** © Mike Slack (from *Pyramids - The Ice Plant*, 2009) / **69** © Duane Michals, Courtesy of D.C. Moore Gallery, New York / **72** © Henri Cartier-Bresson /Magnum Photos / **76** Image courtesy and © Panos Kokkinias / **83** Image courtesy and © Franco Fontana' / **87** *The Three Hags of the Promontory* (*Trí Chailleachaí an Dúna*), www. ameliastein.com / **91** © Alex Webb/Magnum Photos / **94** Courtesy Industry Art / **99** © Sarah Jones, Courtesy Maureen Paley, London / **102** Image courtesy of the artist / **108** © Walker Evans Archive, The Metropolitan Museum of Art, New York / **114** Courtesy the artist and The Approach, London. / **120** Courtesy and © Florencia Durante

Picture research: Peter Kent
Design: Alexandre Coco

Published in 2016 by
Laurence King Publishing Ltd
361–373 City Road
London EC1V 1LR
e-mail: enquiries@laurenceking.com
www.laurenceking.com

Reprinted in 2017 (twice)

© text 2016 Henry Carroll

This book was designed and produced by
Laurence King Publishing Ltd, London.

Henry Carroll has asserted his right under
the Copyright, Designs and Patents Act, 1988,
to be identified as the author of this work.

A catalogue record for this book
is available from the British Library.
ISBN: 978-1-78067-888-7

Printed in China